Published by Creative Education

P.O. Box 227, Mankato, Minnesota 56002

Creative Education is an imprint of The Creative Company

www.thecreativecompany.us

Design by Stephanie Blumenthal

Production by Christine Vanderbeek

Art direction by Rita Marshall

Printed in the United States of America

Photographs by Alamy (Adrian Sherratt, INTERFOTO, Mary Evans Picture Library, Montagu
Images, North Wind Picture Archives, Pictorial Press Ltd, The Print Collector, PRISMA ARCHIVO),
Getty Images (Wolfgang Kaehler, Kean Collection, Bob Thomas/Popperfoto, Universal History Archive),
iStockphoto (Keith Bishop, jpa1999, arne thaysen, Duncan Walker), Mary Evans Picture Library (Mary
Evans, INTERFOTO/Sammlung Rauch), Shutterstock (J. Helgason, Stocksnapper), Superstock (Image
Asset Management Ltd., Pantheon, Universal Images Group)

Library of Congress Cataloging-in-Publication Data

Helget, Nicole Lea.

Barbarians / Nicole Helget.

p. cm. — (Fearsome fighters)

Summary: A compelling look at barbarians, including their clashes with the Greek
and Roman empires, their lifestyle, their weapons, and how they remain a part of
today's culture through books and film.

Includes bibliographical references and index.

ISBN 978-1-60818-182-7

1. Migrations of nations—Juvenile literature. 2. Middle Ages—Juvenile literature.
3. Europe—History—392–814—Juvenile literature. I. Title.

D135.H45 2012

940.1—dc23   2011035798

First edition

2 4 6 8 9 7 5 3 1

BARBARIANS

kaiolus impaint

maginis Annis .1 +.

NICOLE HELGET

FEARSOME FIGHTERS

CREATIVE EDUCATION

From the beginning of time, wherever groups of people have lived together, they have also fought among themselves. Some have fought for control of basic necessities—food, water, and shelter—or territory. Others have been spurred to fight by religious differences. Still others have fought solely for sport. Throughout the ages, some fighters have taken up arms willingly; others have been forced into battle. For all, however, the ultimate goal has always been victory.

Barbarians, historically speaking, were any group of people in ancient times who were not Greek or Roman. The Greeks coined the name to categorize anyone they considered to be uncivilized, and the Romans adopted the term as well. Barbarian tribes fought among themselves and against the armies of the Greek and Roman **empires**, which often instigated war by attacking the barbarians, ransacking their supplies, and enslaving their people. The empires of Greece and Rome—which reigned from about 336 to 30 B.C. and from 27 B.C. to A.D. 476 respectively—would likely have controlled all of Europe if groups of barbarian peoples had not organized and fought back for their share of resources and territories. Ultimately, barbarian fighters helped bring down these empires, forging a legacy as determined and often mysterious battlefield foes.

THE BARBARIANS ARISE

For hundreds of years, two dominant cultures ruled over much of what is now Europe and the Middle East: the Greek Empire and the Roman Empire. Both empires spread in every direction, conquering the small tribes of people who lived in the areas and folding them into their own empire, thereby acquiring new taxpayers and often gaining slave labor. To the Greeks and Romans, the strange languages of these people sounded like "bar, bar, bar," or unintelligible speech, from which came the name "barbarians." Although the term barbarian has carried negative connotations over time, the name has referred to many accomplished cultures over the years. The ancient Greeks called the Persians—people living in present-day Iran—barbarians, though the Persians were an advanced people who had organized their own vast empire. Numerous tribes since the rise of the Roman Empire have been categorized as barbarians, but among the most prominent are the Celts, Franks, Goths, Huns, and Vikings.

People today often picture barbarians as brawny, crazed looters, **arsonists**, and destroyers. In reality, most barbarians were not very physically imposing, nor were they simple-minded and bloodthirsty. In many cases, the people labeled as barbarians fought out of necessity, to protect themselves from the bullying intrusions of dominant empires. The life of a barbarian warrior was hard. Most barbarians **migrated** often and survived on very little food and only occasional shelter. Many barbarian tribes were small, wiry, and often malnourished people. They lived with few comforts and were exposed to all manners of harsh weather, from snow to wind to extreme heat. To survive this difficult lifestyle and endure the onslaught of large, powerful armies, many barbarians relied upon perseverance and their wits more than they did physical strength.

THROUGHOUT MUCH OF HISTORY, BARBARIANS WERE PORTRAYED AS WILD PEOPLES TRYING TO TOPPLE CIVILIZED EMPIRES

The Celts were a group of barbarians who lived in central Europe during the **Iron Age**, eventually concentrating in Britain as the Roman Empire rose to power. The Celts traded goods with the ancient Greeks but clashed with Roman armies after the Roman Empire effectively replaced the Greek Empire around 30 B.C. When Roman soldiers encountered the Celts, they marveled at the barbarians' skill in shaping metal. The Celts used their metalworking to fashion knives and axes for battle and plows and scythes for planting and harvesting. Celts were accomplished builders and farmers, but as the Romans discovered, they were capable of putting up a fierce defense if attacked.

The Franks, a barbarian group of Germanic people who first appeared in recorded history around A.D. 50 in an attack on the Roman Empire, creatively linked their own origins to the legendary city of Troy. The Franks said that their ancestors were among the 12,000 individuals who left Troy after a Greek army captured and destroyed the city. The king of these people was named Francio, which is how both the Franks and modern France got their names. The Franks lived along the Rhine River, then known as the region of Gaul, which was captured and claimed by the Romans in 52 B.C. under governor Julius Caesar (100–44 B.C.). The Franks were masterful artists and craftsmen, and

AN ILLUSTRATION OF ARMED, TRIBAL EUROPEANS—KNOWN TO THE ROMANS AS BARBARIANS—AROUND A.D. 50

$\mathcal{B}$eowulf *is an **epic poem** that tells of the life and exploits of Beowulf, the fictional hero of a barbarian tribe around the 6th century* A.D. *In the story, the warrior Beowulf visits another tribe and offers his assistance in defeating Grendel, a monstrous creature that attacks and eats people in a great hall called Heorot. Beowulf and his men sleep in the hall to confront Grendel. The monster attacks in the black of night and devours one man, then reaches for Beowulf. The hero uses his strength to twist Grendel's arm off, at which point the beast runs away and dies.*

BARBARIANS

many of their creations survive to this day in museums around the world. Intelligent and organized, these barbarians had a reputation for being tenacious fighters as well, and Frankish military leaders were known to organize their troops into efficient battlefield formations and to design clever schemes to outwit their enemies.

The Goths first appeared in recorded history around A.D. 300, when a historian noted a savage invasion of the northern border of the Roman Empire. Before that, various groups of Goths had been wandering around the plains of southern Asia and eastern Europe, where they became skilled horsemen due, in part, to the invention of the stirrup, which made it easier for a rider to control a horse and gallop at high speeds. Even though the stirrup improved safety, it didn't reduce the high mortality rate among the Goths. They were an incredibly combative group of people and often instigated battle with tribes such as the Huns in clashes over land, supplies, or even honor. Such steady warring contributed to a low Gothic population. Perhaps

because they didn't have large numbers, these barbarians had to rely on speed in their warfare.

The Huns were a **nomadic** people who appeared in Europe around A.D. 350. These barbarians were master horsemen and expert archers, and they used these skills to travel widely over mountains and through rivers and canyons, hunting game with their bows and arrows as they went. Even among other barbarian cultures, the Huns were considered to be an especially tough and fearsome people. Historians disagree over where exactly the Huns originated, but most scholars believe they likely came from the harsh and wintry lands near the Volga River in what is now Russia.

Historical accounts suggest the Huns were ugly, cruel, and prideful. Indeed, the Huns practiced a tradition that led to heavily scarred faces. Jordanes, a historian who wrote a book on the barbarian tribes around A.D. 550, noted of the Huns, "They made their foes flee in horror because their swarthy aspect was fearful.... Their hardihood is evident in their wild appearance,

*Barbarian warriors probably adopted the **composite** bow from the Mongol warriors of Asia, and the weapon transformed their ability to fight the Romans. Before that, barbarians used wooden bows, which were relatively weak and inaccurate. Barbarians made composite bows by combining strong wood, bone, animal tendons and muscles, and sticky fish jelly. Such bows were taut and springy, which meant that arrows could be fired at higher velocities, with greater accuracy, and from longer distances than before. It was the composite bow, perhaps more than any other weapon, that helped the barbarian tribes ultimately defeat the Romans.*

and they are beings who are cruel to their children on the very day they are born. For they cut the cheeks of the males with a sword so that before they receive the nourishment of milk they must learn to endure wounds."

Although the Huns were a wandering people, they were able to domesticate animals for food, clothing, and a means of labor. Along with their horses, the Huns kept herds of goats, sheep, and cattle. Very little information remains today about the Hunnic language. Some historians believe Huns spoke a language that was a mixture of Turkish, Mongolian, and Latin, which would be reflective of their wide travels.

The Vikings are sometimes called "The Last Barbarians," as they arose centuries after the fall of the Roman Empire. In the late 700s and early 800s A.D., people living along the western coast of Europe looked over the ocean horizon and saw enormous, colorful sails flapping in

THE HUNS (ABOVE) TRAVELED RUGGED LANDS ON HORSES, WHEREAS THE VIKINGS (OPPOSITE) TRAVERSED THE SEAS ON LONGSHIPS

BARBARIANS

the wind. The sails, attached to huge ships carrying men and women wearing furs and helmets, heralded the landing of the Vikings upon British and French shores. These seafaring people crossed the oceans and seas by way of their masterful shipbuilding, expert navigational skills, and sheer determination, and they landed in a wave of hollering and swinging axes. Hailing from the Scandinavian countries of Denmark, Finland, Iceland, Norway, and Sweden, the Vikings became known as feared barbarian raiders to coastal peoples. These "Northmen" could be brutal and violent as they seized slaves and treasure, but they were also interested in exploring, trading, and settling new regions.

ARROWS, SWORDS, AND BLUDGEONING BALLS

The weapons wielded by barbarian warriors differed considerably by tribe, varying according to the lifestyles and traditions of each. The Celts would hurl stones over vast distances by using slings made of tree branches and string made from animal skin or guts. With these simple instruments, the Celts could propel stones farther and with more damaging velocities than if they were only throwing them. An enemy approaching a Celtic village might be ambushed by a hail of rocks.

Celtic warriors, however, truly excelled in close-quarters fighting. When engaging an enemy in hand-to-hand combat, Celtic warriors used spears and swords, stabbing at their opponent's heart and slicing at exposed limbs. The Celts made spears out of long strips of wood and then tipped them with an iron or bronze spearhead. They had two types of spears. A sturdier, stouter version was used in up-close fighting, while a longer, slimmer version was hurled through the air for long-range attacks. Any Celtic warrior could wield a spear, but fighters who were older, more experienced, or more respected carried a spear some 20 to 30 inches (51–76 cm) longer and made entirely of iron. Some warriors had yet longer and heavier spears that had to be managed with two hands, but such weapons were rare and the property of only the most expert warriors or revered Celtic leaders. While the Celts did use shields to protect their bodies, traditional lore and some historical accounts portray the Celts as nude or nearly nude fighters. Charging into battle clad in little more than their bare skin might have been a display of unity with their clansmen or an effort to strike fear or disbelief into the enemy.

The Franks used their rich stores of metals to **smelt** swords, shields, arrow tips, and axes. Frankish warriors also often deployed bludgeon-

THESE CELTIC WARRIORS, WEARING MORE CLOTHING THAN WAS CUSTOMARY IN BATTLE, CARRY SWORDS AND SPEARS

BARBARIANS

ing balls, which were heavy metal spheres attached to chains. A skilled Frankish warrior could swing the bludgeoning ball and then smash it into his enemy, causing catastrophic injuries. But perhaps more than any physical item they wielded, the Franks' most powerful weapon was their ability to work together and quickly build settlements and fortresses to protect themselves from invading armies. These fortresses gave the Franks a secure place to settle and prepare for coming attacks. Their walled cities also provided a measure of safety for vulnerable women, children, and elderly people while the male warriors were away fighting. Historians would later write about the architectural beauty and the elegant carvings of the buildings inside such forts, which demonstrated the Franks' appreciation for art.

Famed for their horsemanship, the Goths were also skilled carpenters, a craft they used to create horse carts for use in battle. A rider guided the horse pulling the cart, while warriors in the cart launched arrows from a position of relative safety. The Goths also used swords, spears, and shields at close quarters. These barbarians were known for using fire as a weapon of war, setting fire to huts, tents, and other structures to

drive the enemy out or to wipe out encampments as they retreated. Because food storage units were often destroyed in this way, the effects of a Gothic attack could be felt by an enemy long after a battle. Without sufficient food, famine would set in, further disabling the enemy.

Like their Gothic counterparts, the Huns are remembered for their ability to fight while mounted as well as for their expertise with the bow and arrow. To an enemy facing a Hun onslaught, the mounted barbarians likely seemed to be everywhere at once, so skillful, fast, and organized were their attacks. Because speed was pivotal in the Huns' attack, they did not wear heavy or cumbersome armor or leather tunics. Instead, they fought in their everyday clothing, which typically consisted of a pair of coarse pants, a shirt, and a vest or coat. Huns did not carry shields or other heavy weapons. This was partly because they needed to keep their hands free to draw arrows from their quivers to their bows and because they did not want extra weight to slow their horses.

A Hunnic warrior may have wielded a sword during close encounters, but only part of a Hun army would have been outfitted with

*I*f it weren't for the efforts of Jordanes—a historian who recorded the events of the 6th-century world around him—very little would be known about the barbarian cultures, since many of them had no written language at all. Roman writers were dutiful **propagandists**, which meant they recorded history in a light favorable to their own empire. Jordanes, a man of both Gothic and Roman descent, wrote The Origin and Deeds of the Goths *around* A.D. 550, offering a fair and historically authentic look at life among the barbarians.

them. The Huns depended upon a quick volley of arrows to deplete the enemy ranks before engaging in hand-to-hand combat. The barbarians were as protective of their horses' lives as they were of their own. Aside from the saddle upon which the rider sat, the horse's hide was bare, which let the animal maneuver easily but also left it exposed to enemy attacks during a battle. The Hun warrior had to be fast and clever to minimize the risk of having his horse shot by arrows or otherwise maimed.

The Huns were quick learners on the battlefield, taking note of the attack strategies of opposing armies. They were also known to shift their allegiances. Although Hun barbarians long waged war against the Romans, the Huns sometimes fought alongside Roman armies and against other barbarian tribes. They traded their time and skill for food, textiles, and money, becoming mercenaries. From these joint campaigns with the Romans, the Huns learned Roman strategies of attack and gained access to useful new weapons such as battering rams.

Unlike many earlier barbarian peoples, the Vikings went into battle heavily armed and armored. On their heads sat helmets of iron. Most Vikings owned a simple cup-shaped helmet, but some warriors wore helmets more intricate in their design. Some helmets had nose protectors hanging from the middle of the front side. Others had a goggle-like apparatus meant to protect the eyes. And some had those features in addition to neck flaps that hung to the shoulders. Although Viking warriors are often depicted in popular culture as wearing helmets with horns that curved upward, no historical evidence exists that the Vikings ever sported horned helmets on a regular basis.

Vikings went into battle carrying heavy axes, shields, and broadswords, but their greatest weapon was the longship, a sturdy vessel that carried the warriors across seas and through shallow rivers to their destinations. The Vikings were able to penetrate territories unconquerable by other groups because of their ships' speed and range. A Viking ship was often decorated with a carved, wooden dragon head mounted on the **prow** and was powered across the water both by oars and by square sails that were usually plain or striped in appearance.

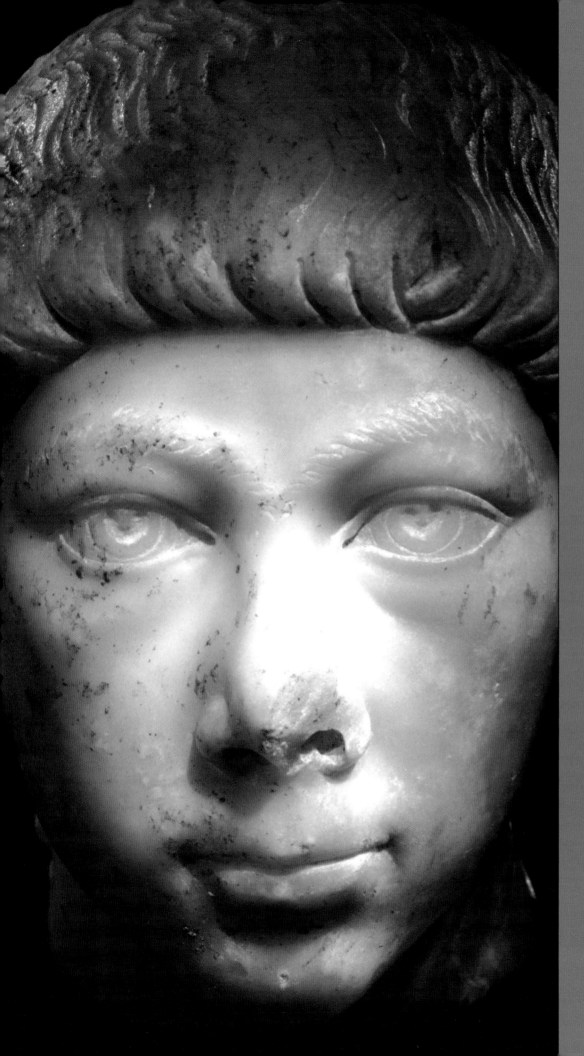

In A.D. 378, when news of a humiliating military defeat at the Turkish city of Adrianople reached the Roman emperor Gratian, he wanted revenge for the death of his uncle and co-emperor Valens, who was slain on the battlefield by an army of Gothic horsemen. So, Gratian ordered the slaughter of thousands of Gothic children. The massacre so enraged the Goths and other barbarians that they began launching persistent and violent attacks on Rome. The loss at Adrianople and the death of the innocents marked the beginning of the end for the Roman Empire, which would ultimately collapse under the onslaught of barbarian invasions.

A STATUE OF THE ROMAN EMPEROR GRATIAN

AMBUSHES AND ADAPTATIONS

In contrast to the huge, well-supported, and systematic armies of the Greek and Roman empires, barbarian warriors were few in number, had limited resources, and were unconventional in their tactics. Whereas imperial armies often marched into battle in formations consisting of efficient and unrelenting rows of soldiers, barbarians improvised, relying on ambush attacks and fast raids. While they could rarely match their enemies in terms of numbers and training, barbarians sometimes had the advantage when it came to their ability to create chaos, instill fear in their enemies, and persist through grim circumstances. Perhaps the most important quality possessed by the barbarian warrior was his love of family, tribe, or culture. Whereas the ranks of Greek or Roman armies sometimes included slaves or mercenaries, the barbarian warrior fought for the rights and survival of his wife and children, and ownership of his house and fields. This fact undoubtedly con-tributed to the barbarians' reputation as ferocious fighters. A battlefield victory for the average Greek soldier or Roman legionnaire might mean little more than a brief rest before the next march and battle. Victory for a barbarian warrior meant freedom and the retention of his way of life.

Many barbarian battles originated with an ambush, which sometimes was planned weeks, months, or even years in advance. Oftentimes, to gain an informational advantage, the barbarians would embed a spy in the ranks of their enemies. Because Greek and Roman armies often hired soldiers or forced slaves to fight for the empire, it was not unusual to find **infantry** of many different nationalities among the imperial ranks. As a member of this army, a barbarian spy could gain access to an army's preferred fighting techniques or future plans of attack. He could then relay this knowledge to his people to help them prepare for battles to come.

GERMANIC BARBARIANS AMBUSHING A ROMAN LEGION

*W*ith the end of the Roman Empire came land and power grabs by barbarian rulers. Among the Franks, Charlemagne (747–814) arose to become one of the most influential kings in European history. Charlemagne, who was of Germanic and Frankish descent, united many fractured territories in Europe and spread art and literacy among his people. Through these measures, he also spread Christianity, which eventually led to a worldwide **dissemination** of the religion. Charlemagne himself, however, did not adhere strictly to all Christian teachings, producing more than 20 children with 8 different women.

In some cases, spying barbarian warriors earned enough respect within an imperial army that they could affect its plans—persuading enemy troops, for example, to take a certain path or **rendezvous** at a particular location, all the while guiding them toward a trap. Then, when the imperial army followed such an ill-advised route, barbarian warriors would attack, emerging out of the trees or from behind rocks to assault the army before it had time to form effective lines of defense. In some cases, the barbarians would take advantage of the natural features of the land, appearing suddenly atop a ridge and descending upon opponents who were trapped in a valley. Since a barbarian army might have half the troops—or even fewer—of imperial armies, barbarians valued the element of surprise.

Another defining characteristic of the barbarian warrior was his ability to move steadily and adapt to new locations. Barbarian tribes were used to living outdoors, and many were **transient** people. If a barbarian army had to travel to a distant border to protect it from invasion, women and children would often accompany the warriors, bringing along all they owned—herds of livestock, food, farming tools, and shelters. The armies of Greece and Rome were often away from home for many months, if not years, at a time.

A LOOKOUT KEEPING WATCH FOR APPROACHING ROMANS

BARBARIANS

After a fierce day of fighting, these soldiers could not return home to their wives and children and eat a home-cooked meal in the way the barbarian warrior could. Unlike their supposedly more "civilized" enemies, barbarian warriors had little separation between family and fighting, and they considered home to be wherever they happened to be camping at that time.

Although usually not as well-armed as their enemies, when it came to battle, barbarian fighters were quick to take action and adept at maximizing the limited resources available to them. Lookouts called spotters were charged with watching for invading armies. If a spotter saw an army on the move toward his camp or village, he would ride back and give warning. Then the barbarians could begin to prepare for the invasion. They would sometimes send the women and children to protected areas in mountains or other areas of greater safety. If enemies were closing in and the barbarians didn't have time, the tribes might move vulnerable members to the center of the village. Then the warriors might arrange their carts and wagons, if they possessed them, to encircle the village to form a protective outer barrier.

From behind this barrier, the warriors could hurl rocks or launch arrows or spears at the invaders.

In some cases, barbarian warriors would set fire to their own fields, in which they might be growing crops such as wheat. If the wind was right, the smoke would drift into enemy soldiers, disorienting and temporarily blinding them. Greek or Roman soldiers were often dressed in armor or **chain mail**, which was heavy and hot. As these soldiers drew closer, the heat of a fire could overwhelm them, halting their advance. As the smoke and heat disrupted the typically uniform lines of enemy archers, **cavalry**, and infantry, barbarian warriors—with the protection of their makeshift barriers—would pick off the weary soldiers emerging out of the smoke.

Many barbarian warriors engaged in a kind of psychological warfare through their physical appearance. Greek and Roman soldiers looked impressive in their colored uniforms, clanking armor, and perhaps shiny chain mail; barbarian warriors, by contrast, often looked downright crazy. The warriors of some tribes, including the Celts, might have fought naked, with their lack of clothing suggesting a fearless-

Today, when property is destroyed or marked with graffiti, we say it has been "vandalized," or defaced by "vandals." The word "vandal" comes from a group of barbarians that sacked Rome in A.D. 455. The Vandals originated in the region today called Germany, but due to pressure from the Huns, they were forced out of their native lands. They moved into Gaul, Frankish territory, which is the area now composed of France, Belgium, and Luxembourg. The Vandals emerged as a formidable fighting people there and later invaded Italy, where they were memorialized in history as destroyers of property, forever linking their name with the act.

ness that stunned their enemies. Among other barbarian tribes that did not go entirely unclothed, fighting attire varied from one warrior to the next.

Barbarian fighters enhanced their prowess as warriors by way of masterful storytelling, too. Although the ability to tell a story well might seem a curious asset in warfare, the barbarians found a way to put it to their advantage. Barbarian warriors spread tales of their wartime exploits that portrayed them as merciless and wicked. Roman soldiers heard tales of barbarians **eviscerating** their captured enemies, burning buildings filled with women and children, and propping severed heads on stakes. They came to fear barbarian tortures that might include the plucking out of eyeballs and the removal of tongues. Wherever the barbarians went, they spread stories of their own cruelty, thereby planting seeds of fear and weakening the confidence of soldiers they might meet on the field of battle.

THE VICTORS IN CLASHES BETWEEN BARBARIAN AND ROMAN FORCES FREQUENTLY BEHEADED THEIR CAPTIVE FOES

FROM ARMINIUS TO ATTILA

Because the barbarian name encompasses numerous tribes that were spread throughout **Eurasia** and across a time span of more than a millennium, many barbarian leaders have staked prominent places in the history of warfare. Many were men, but some were women. Among the first of these famous leaders was Arminius (c. 18 B.C.–A.D. 19). Known as the Teutonic Warrior, Arminius was a member of a tribe called the Cherusci that battled against the Roman Empire. Under Arminius's rule, the tribe was able to halt the advance of the Romans by destroying several **legions** in the Teutoburg Forest (in present-day Germany) by leading them there and then slaughtering them in A.D. 9. The Roman general Varus was so humiliated by the defeat that he fell upon his sword and committed suicide rather than live with the shame.

Despite his brilliant military tactics, Arminius was undone by the treachery of his own people—particularly that of his father-in-law Segestes, a noble among the Teutonic tribe who secretly aligned himself with the Romans. In an effort to secure long-term safety for himself after the Roman defeat in the Teutoburg Forest, Segestes gave his daughter—Arminius's wife—and son over to the Romans. Roman officials showed them off in "victory" parades in which they tried to convince their citizens that they had control of the Teutonic barbarians.

While in captivity, Arminius's wife gave birth to his child, a son he would never know. With his daughter out of the way, Segestes was able to orchestrate the assassination of Arminius, who was slain under mysterious circumstances. Arminius's son Thumelicus was made to live among the Romans as a slave, forced into the life of a gladiator. He died fighting for the thrill of the Roman citizens while a young man. Arminius is remembered today as Hermann the German, a

ARMINIUS IS HOISTED ALOFT IN CELEBRATION AFTER DEFEATING VARUS IN THE BATTLE OF THE TEUTOBURG FOREST

In 1930, an American writer named Robert E. Howard dreamed up a new character for the reading public. That character, Conan the Barbarian—a muscular, barely-clothed warrior—would inspire toys, movie characters, bodybuilding contests, strongman competitions, and video games for decades to come. Conan the Barbarian first appeared in print as a character in a Howard short story published in the magazine Weird Tales in June 1932. The character reappeared in numerous stories and poems after that, and later authors, filmmakers, and cartoonists adapted Howard's tales for their own purposes.

hero to many of his descendants and an example of German strength.

By about A.D. 60, after centuries of Celtic-Roman conflict, the Celts had fallen largely under the power of Rome, with the empire exerting control over their homeland (present-day Great Britain and Ireland). On his deathbed, a Celtic tribal king named Prasutagus (d. A.D. 60)—hoping to leave his wife Boudicca (d. A.D. 60), two teenage daughters, and people with a semblance of peace—signed half of his lands over to the Romans. The Romans, though, were dissatisfied by this gesture. They thought that Queen Boudicca, the Celts' new leader, would be easily defeated and that the remaining Celtic lands would soon be theirs. The Romans captured Boudicca, and in an effort to degrade her, soldiers **flogged** her in front of her people and raped her daughters. The Romans thought this public humiliation would convince her to submit and surrender her people's lands, but the queen refused to yield. Instead, she began hatching a plan for revenge.

As Boudicca healed from her wounds, she rallied the support of neighboring Celtic tribes and organized an ambush on the Roman army. When the Romans caught wind of a planned rebellion, they sent troops from Colchester, a Roman stronghold. But Boudicca and her Celtic warriors lay in wait along a dark road, and as the Roman army marched into position, the barbar-

BOUDICCA STANDS BEFORE HER WEEPING, DISHONORED DAUGHTERS AS SHE COMMANDS HER CELTIC WARRIORS

ians swarmed upon them and slaughtered them. Still, the victory was not enough for Boudicca. She and her army—made up of as many as 100,000 warriors—marched on to Colchester and London and attacked. They destroyed most of the cities, including Colchester's famous temple to the emperor Claudius, and annihilated most of the population within their borders—as many as 70,000 people, by some estimates. Knowing the Roman Empire would not rest until it had captured and either killed her or exhibited her as a political trophy, Boudicca took her own life after this vengeful victory by drinking poison.

Alaric I (c. A.D. 370–410), a Goth, was another leader who carved out a prominent place in the annals of barbarian history. As a young man, Alaric dreamed that he would one day capture the city of Rome—the heart of the Roman Empire. In A.D. 410, he did just that. Twenty-eight years before, the Goths had actually come to the Romans for help. The Huns had pushed the Goths out of their lands and were threatening to annihilate them, so the Goths went to the Roman emperor and requested an alliance. The empire allowed the Goths to settle along the Danube River, and

ALARIC I LIVED ONLY 40 YEARS BUT CHANGED EUROPE

$\mathcal{T}$he role of women in Celtic culture was a rough one. Not only were women responsible for feeding men and birthing and caring for children, but sometimes they were also responsible for participating in battle. One historian wrote, "The work which the best women had to do was to go to battle and battlefield … fighting and hosting, wounding and slaying. On one side of her she would carry her bag of provisions, on the other her babe." In A.D. 697, the Law of Innocents, a set of rules for warfare created by a Celtic religious leader named Adomnán, was established to attempt to protect women and children.

the barbarians fought alongside the Romans against the Huns. The Romans, though, began taking advantage of their Gothic guests and helped themselves to the Goths' resources, such as food and cloth. Alaric grew tired of the mistreatment and devised a plan to topple the emperor's army and claim the city for himself. He launched several assaults on Rome, finally capturing the city in 410. He was a great lover of art and beauty, so instead of burning the entire city, as many barbarians would have preferred, he left many of its artful buildings standing.

The Romans referred to Attila the Hun (d. A.D. 453) as "The Scourge of God," so feared was he for his relentless and seemingly fearless attacks on Roman armies, settlements, and cities. Historical accounts of Attila vary, with some depicting him as a wise, inspiring warrior and others portraying him as a terrible, **cannibalistic** monster. The truth is probably somewhere in between. Around A.D. 434, Attila shared the title of king of the Huns with his brother, Bleda (c. A.D. 390–445), after the death of their uncle. Until that time, Hun clans were disorganized and fought amongst themselves. Attila united the clans and encouraged them to work together to defeat the Roman army as well as other barbarian armies.

Under the brothers' leadership, the Huns were victorious in notable battles against the Romans and barbarian tribes who were allied with the Romans in Gaul and Italy. Attila later likely orchestrated the death of his brother, making it appear to be a hunting accident, and took the throne for himself.

As the sole leader of the Huns, Attila captured more than 100 Roman cities and earned a terrifying reputation by killing thousands of enemies and—by his own admission—eating some of his victims. Although it is uncertain whether he actually ate people, the mere suggestion of cannibalism was enough to give pause to enemies who were considering attacking Attila's army. The Huns emerged as one of the most powerful barbarian tribes in history under Attila, but his reign was brief. On the night of his wedding, Attila drank heavily. As he slept in his tent, he suffered a nosebleed, which caused him to choke on his own blood. At least, this was the story given to Attila's loyal subjects. Some historians have speculated that his new bride was involved in a scheme to remove him from power and that she killed him in his sleep.

HISTORICAL RECORDS SUGGEST THAT ATTILA THE HUN WAS A SHORT, STRONG MAN WITH A LARGE HEAD AND SMALL EYES

DOMESTICATION OF THE BARBARIANS

The Migration Period, also known as the Barbarian Invasions, was a time characterized by widespread movement of various tribal peoples throughout Europe from around A.D. 300 to 900. During this period, one tribe and then another packed up and moved to seek shelter and food, fighting with other tribes and with Roman soldiers for these resources along the way. The migrations of the Huns, Goths, Franks, and many other groups—and their repeated invasions into Roman territory—led to the collapse of the western part of the Roman Empire (the eastern portion of the empire, called the Byzantine Empire, would retain much of its strength until the 1400s).

The period that overlapped with and followed this is often called the Dark Ages, because so little art and literature were created during this time. Life for people in the Dark Ages, which lasted from about A.D. 500 to 1100, was difficult, as warfare was widespread, many formerly great urban cities fell into disarray, and mortality rates were high. As the Roman Empire crumbled, barbarian peoples still squabbled over territories and resources until, finally, a semblance of order took shape. By around A.D. 800, most of the barbarian cultures had quit wandering, settled into specific regions, and begun developing their own stable cities, roads, and governments. In short, the barbarians became domesticated.

Celtic culture gave rise to the flourishing territories of Scotland, Ireland, Brittany, Cornwall, Wales, and the Isle of Man. The Franks settled present-day France and parts of Spain and Italy. The Goths affected the settlement of Sweden, Poland, Moldova, Ukraine, and other modern eastern European countries. The Huns and other Germanic tribes left their mark on present-day Austria, Germany, the Netherlands, Belgium, and England. And Viking culture turned

FRANKISH PEOPLE MIGRATING ACROSS THE RHINE RIVER

into the modern settlement of Norway, Denmark, Finland, and Sweden.

For centuries, barbarian peoples were saddled with a grim reputation, the very word "barbarian" bringing to mind a cruel and unintelligent brute with blood on his hands and a crude sword dangling from his side. But the barbarian tribes were mostly victims of the powerful propaganda machine of the Roman Empire, which used its wealth and influence to write history to suit its own purposes. So, while the Roman Empire was invading barbarian lands and pillaging tribal villages, Roman **scribes** recorded those events as if the empire had liberated or enlightened a foreign people. In more recent years, this one-sided perspective has changed. Historians continue to study the writings of the Romans but with greater attention paid to the barbarian point of view.

While the various barbarian tribes did away with their nomadic, warring ways long ago, barbarians continue to loom large in popular culture in all sorts of ways. The Vikings, for example, are prominently featured in modern culture and entertainment. Sports teams capitalize on the fierce reputation of these warriors of the North, with clubs such as the Minnesota Vikings of the National Football League taking the Viking as

AN IMAGE OF A ROMAN SCRIBE RECORDING HISTORY

Historians struggle to pinpoint what inspired the massive migratory movement of the barbarians starting in the 4th century A.D. Some speculate that climate changes compelled the groups to move, which generated conflicts as tribes entered already claimed territories. The eruption of the Krakatoa volcano in present-day Indonesia in A.D. 535 spewed massive amounts of ash into the sky, which blocked enough sunlight to lead to a cooling period in that area of the world. The Mongols, a tribe that originated in central Asia, were compelled to move westward into the territories of barbarian tribes, triggering a domino effect of migration.

their name and mascot. In many cities around the world, people gather annually to reenact and celebrate Viking life with annual fairs and festivals.

Today, Celtic influences—especially those relating to religion—are felt in many places around the world. Collectors of jewelry or sculpture might add elaborate images of trees and knots—natural symbols common in the Celtic tradition—to their holdings. All over the world, people gather to celebrate traditional Celtic holidays such as Ostara, which falls after the **spring equinox** in the same way the Christian holiday of Easter does. In fact, many of the traditional religious holidays celebrated by modern Christians began as old, **pagan** Celtic holidays.

The Hun barbarians have lived on by way of films and legend. In 1998, Huns appeared in a Disney animated movie as an invading army threatening the peace of a Chinese village in *Mulan*. The Huns of the movie, in many ways, embody the traditional stereotype of violent marauders and senseless destroyers. Although long having passed into history, the Huns found a way to play a role in 20th-century warfare. In 1900, Kaiser Wilhelm II, the emperor of Germany, encouraged his armies to attack with-

out mercy against the fighters of the Boxer Rebellion—Chinese warriors who fought to keep **Western**, Christian influences from infiltrating China. The kaiser said, "Just as a thousand years ago, the Huns under Attila won a reputation of might that lives on in legends, so may the name of Germany in China." The German soldiers and their allies defeated the Boxer rebels.

Gothic influence, too, has enjoyed a revival in recent years that is apparent in clothing, books, movies, and music. Dark clothes, black lipstick and fingernail polish, and black-dyed hair all make a nod to the Gothic barbarian culture. While such stylistic features do not directly suggest the appearance of the original Goths, this Gothic **subculture** is meant to draw a parallel to the Goths, who—like the modern subculture—didn't fit in with "civilized" society and wanted to choose their own paths. Popular movies such as *Sleepy Hollow*, *Beetlejuice*, and *Edward Scissorhands*—all created by filmmaker Tim Burton—feature Gothic characters who are portrayed as societal outcasts.

The Franks have enjoyed a more positive legacy than other barbarians. This is mostly due to the famous Frankish king Charlemagne, who

A MODERN PAGAN CELEBRATION OF THE SPRING EQUINOX

embraced Christianity and united many of the tribes in present-day France and Germany to challenge the Roman Empire and became, in 800, the Holy Roman emperor. Because the Catholic Church—a very powerful and influential institution—was prolific in its creation of historical writings and records, it chronicled the life and deeds of Charlemagne in a glowing way, which helped improve the reputation of all Franks.

Barbarians of all kinds have made for fascinating subjects on television, computer, and movie screens. In 2006, Terry Jones, a famous British actor, narrated a four-part television series called *Barbarians*, which attempts to clear the barbarian name in history and work as a counterpoint to Roman-authored history. The documentary—based on historical research—paints a picture of barbarians as clever, resourceful, and family-oriented people who could fight fiercely when they had to. The History Channel has also chronicled the lives of Franks, Goths, Huns, Vandals, Vikings, and other tribes in the series *Barbarians* and *Barbarians II*.

Video games such as *Barbarians*, *Viking Warlord*, and *Rome: Total War* allow players to navigate the barbarian world by controlling virtual warriors and weapons. Barbarians have also appeared on the silver screen in many famous movies ranging from 1982's *Conan the Barbarian*, which stars famous bodybuilder-turned-politician Arnold Schwarzenegger, to 2000's *Gladiator*, which depicts barbarians meeting Roman troops in an epic battle.

Barbarians, in all their different embodiments, have earned their place among the world's most famous fighters. As resilient and diverse warriors who resisted—and ultimately helped topple—some of the most powerful empires the world has ever known, barbarians were once the very image of savagery but have been celebrated in more recent years for their resourcefulness and fighting courage as "underdogs" to mighty foes. From the wild lands of Europe and Asia many centuries ago to the screens, books, and legends of today, the spirit of these free and fierce fighters lives on.

Charlemagne holds a sword and a cross, symbolizing his fighting legacy and Catholic conversion

𝒰p until the Battle of Adrianople in A.D. 378, the Roman army achieved one victory after another, thanks to huge numbers of foot soldiers who advanced across battlefields with mathematical precision. At Adrianople, however, the barbarian Goths demonstrated the power of the mounted soldier like never before. Although the opposing armies each numbered about 50,000 troops, the Romans featured mostly infantry, while the Goth forces consisted almost entirely of cavalry. The battle was a massacre, with the Goths riding over and through the Roman ranks. Historians credit this battle with altering military history, as cavalry would become the world's most dominant fighting force over the next 1,000 years.

GLOSSARY

arsonists—People who deliberately set fire to houses or other personal property

cannibalistic—Describing a person or animal that eats other humans or animals of the same species

cavalry—Soldiers who fight on horseback; historically, the most mobile of combat units

chain mail—A protective suit consisting of thousands of tiny metal loops linked meticulously together

composite—Made up of unrelated or separate parts that are brought together

dissemination—The spreading or scattering of a thing or idea

empires—Major political units or countries that have wide-spread territory or a number of territories or peoples under a single authority

epic poem—A long poem that tells the story of a hero's deeds

Eurasia—Europe and Asia when considered together as one continent

eviscerating—Removing the entrails, or guts, from a person or animal

flogged—Beaten with a whip or stick, usually as a means of punishment

infantry—Soldiers trained, armed, and equipped to fight on foot

Iron Age—A period from about 500 B.C. to A.D. 100 marked by the increased use of weapons and utensils made of iron

legions—Divisions of the Roman army usually consisting of 3,000 to 6,000 soldiers

migrated—Moved from one country, region, or place to another, often to find food or work

nomadic—Describing a person who has no permanent home but rather moves from place to place, often to graze livestock

pagan—Describing people who hold religious belief in a god or gods other than the Christian, Muslim, or Jewish god

propagandists—People who publicly spread information, ideas, or rumors as a means of helping or harming a person or group

prow—The forward part of a ship's hull, especially the portion that extends out above the water

rendezvous—To assemble or meet at an agreed time and place

scribes—Writers or authors, especially those who made copies of manuscripts before the invention of the printing press

smelt—To fuse or melt iron

spring equinox—The first time in a year when the sun crosses the plane of Earth's equator, making night and day approximately the same length; it usually occurs around March 20

subculture—A group that has behaviors, appearances, or beliefs distinctive enough to distinguish it from others within the same culture or society

transient—A person or thing that changes locations frequently

Western—Describing the part of the world that includes the United States and Europe

INDEX

BIBLIOGRAPHY

Barbarians. DVD. Directed by Clancy Brown. 2004. New York: A&E Home Video, 2004.

Bury, J. B. *The Invasion of Europe by the Barbarians*. New York: W. W. Norton, 2000.

Cunliffe, Barry. *Greeks, Romans, and Barbarians: Spheres of Interaction*. New York: Methuen Press, 1988.

Goffart, Walter. *Barbarian Tides: The Migration Age and the Later Roman Empire*. Philadelphia: University of Pennsylvania Press, 2006.

Heather, Peter J. *Empires and Barbarians: The Fall of Rome and the Birth of Europe*. New York: Oxford University Press, 2010.

Kelly, Christopher. *The End of Empire: Attila the Hun and the Fall of Rome*. New York: W. W. Norton, 2009.

Terry Jones' Barbarians. DVD. Produced by David McNabb. 2006. London: Oxford Film and Television Production, 2006.

Ward-Perkins, Bryan. *The Fall of Rome: And the End of Civilization*. Oxford: Oxford University Press, 2005.